How to Draw
Super Cute Animals

Copyrighted Material

Cat

Dog

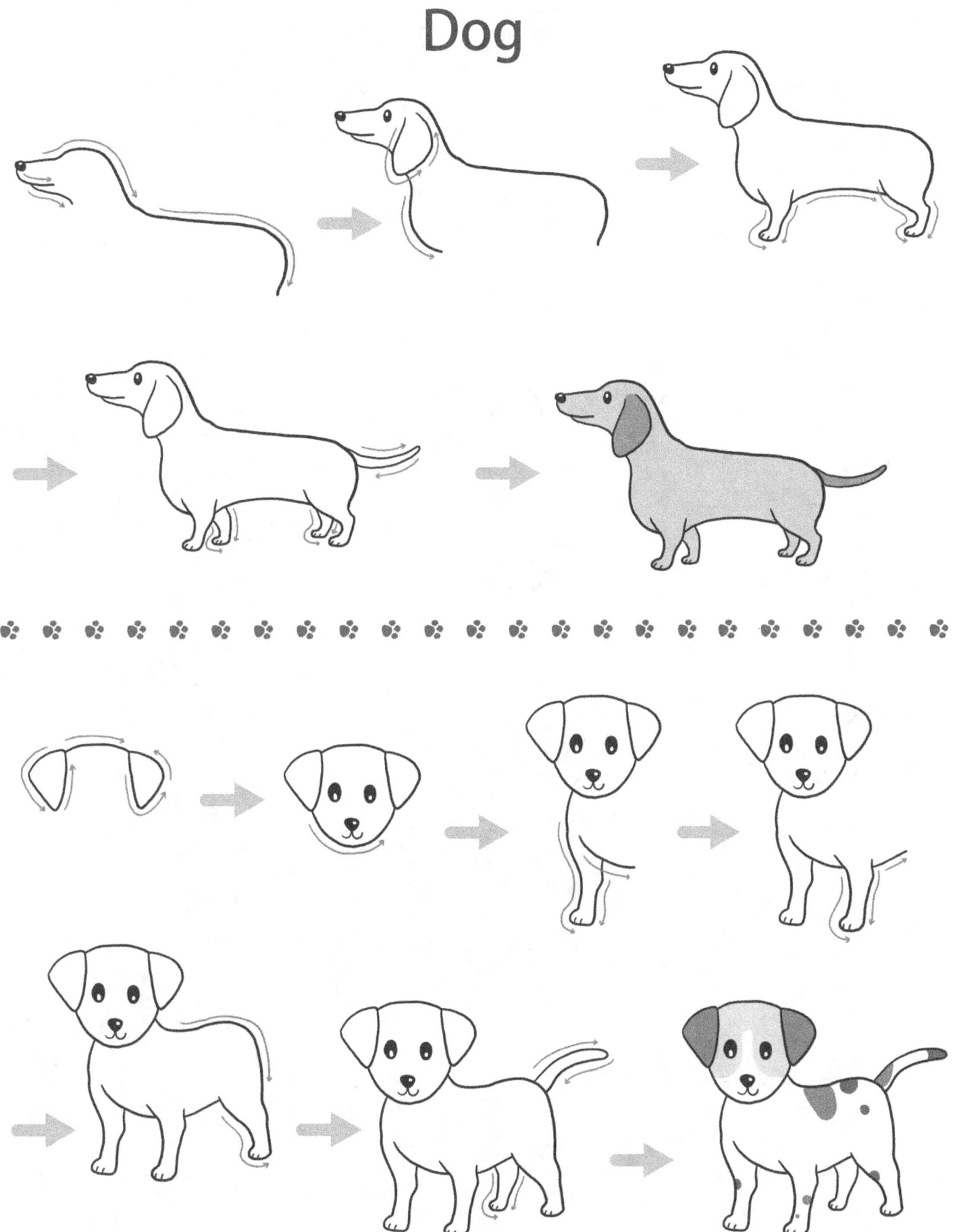

Rabbit

Mouse

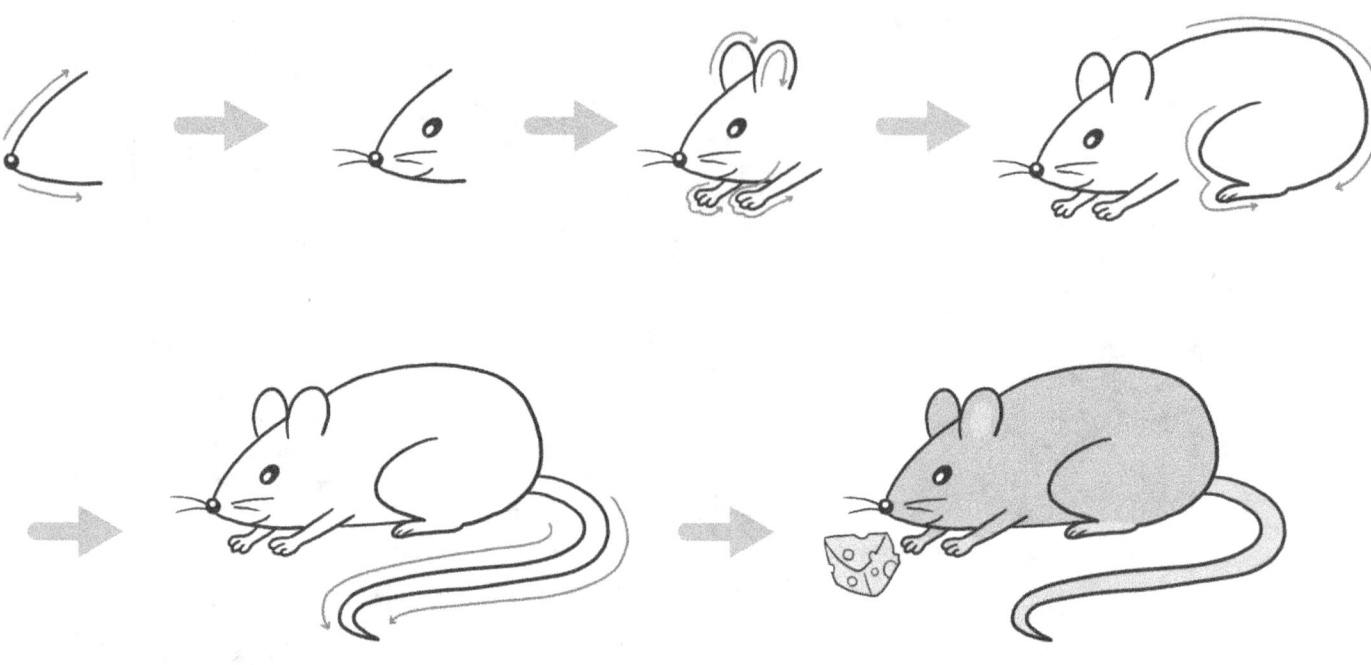

Bat

Raccoon

Skunk

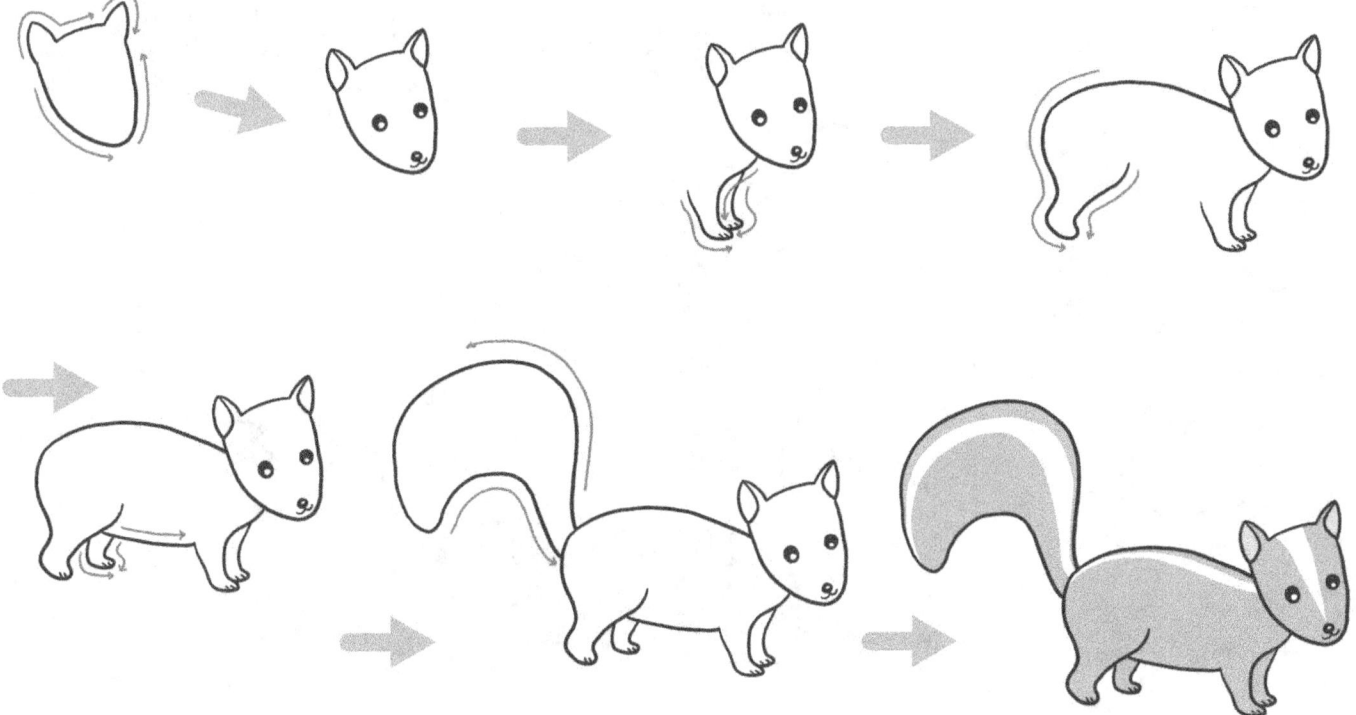

Sheep

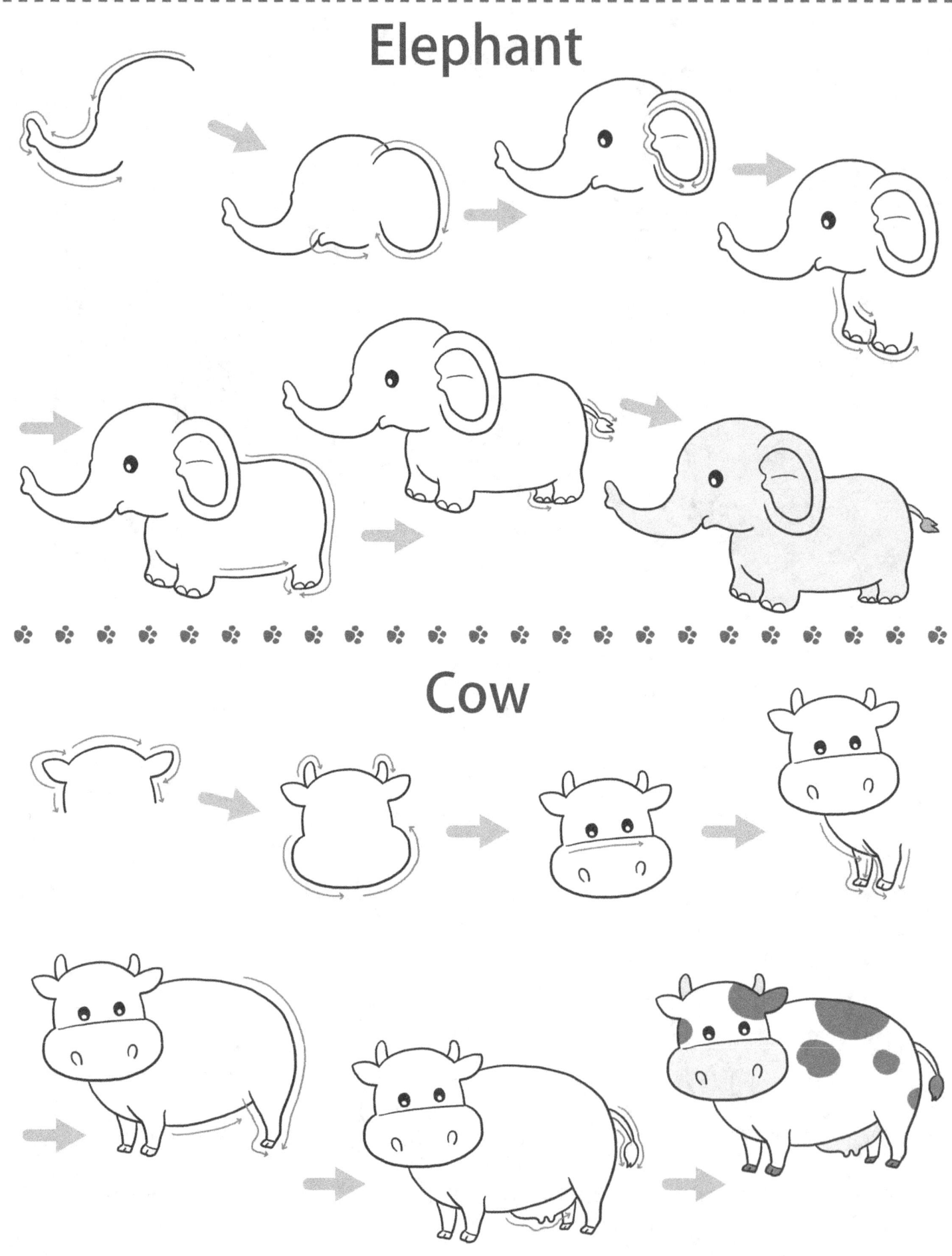

Monkey

Orangutan

Deer

Giraffe

Alpaca

Camel

Bear

Panda

Wolf

Leopard

Rhinoceros

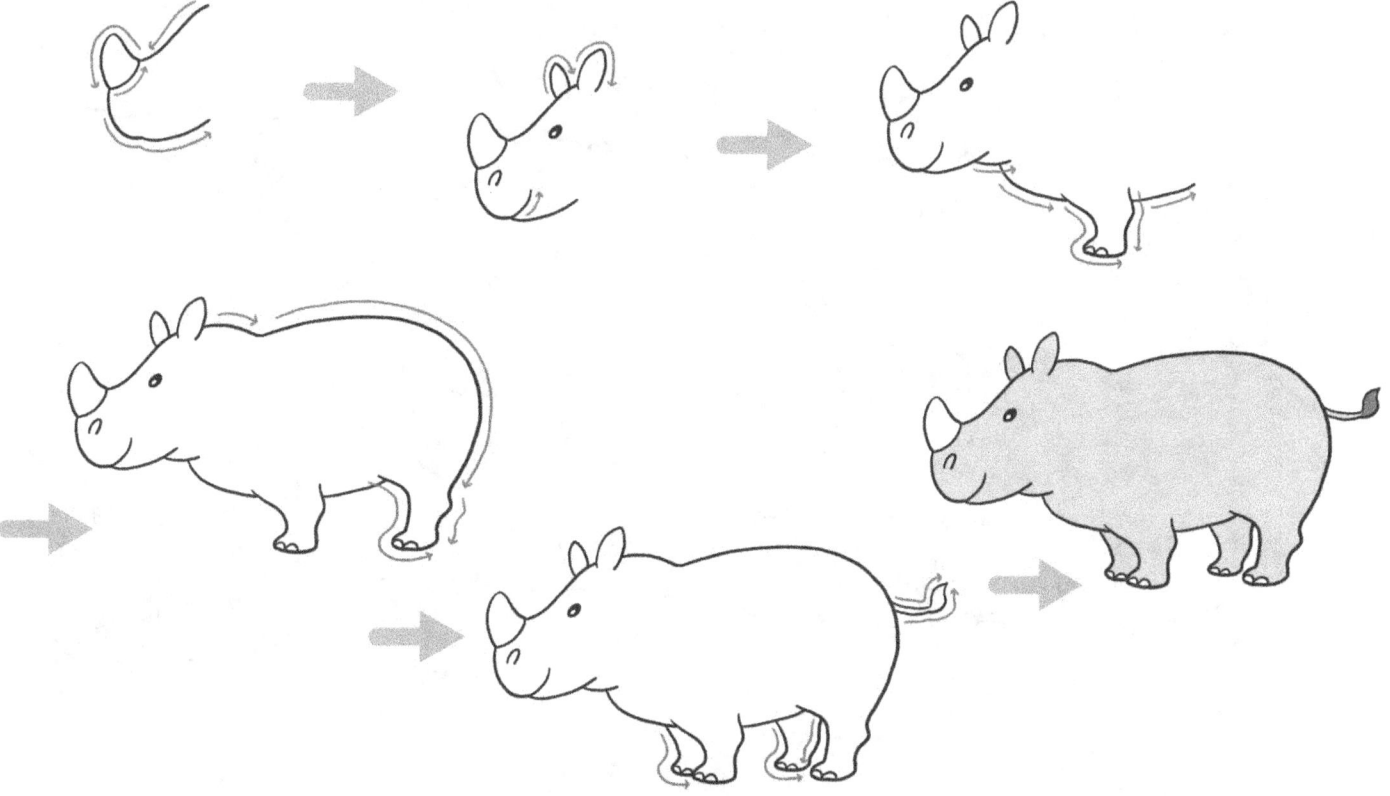

Hippo

Koala

Kangaroo

Sloth

Hedgehog

Anteater

malayan tapir

Duck

Swan

Stork

Owl

Crow

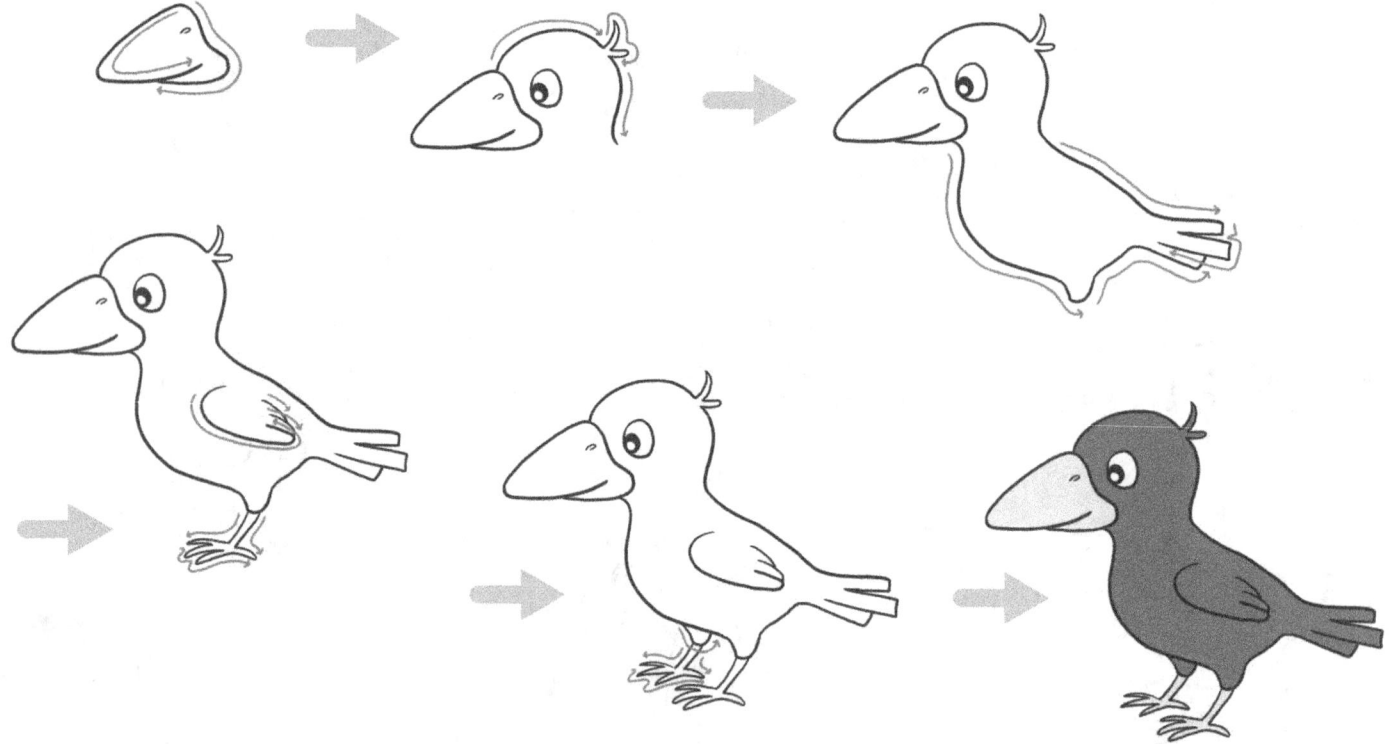

Penguin

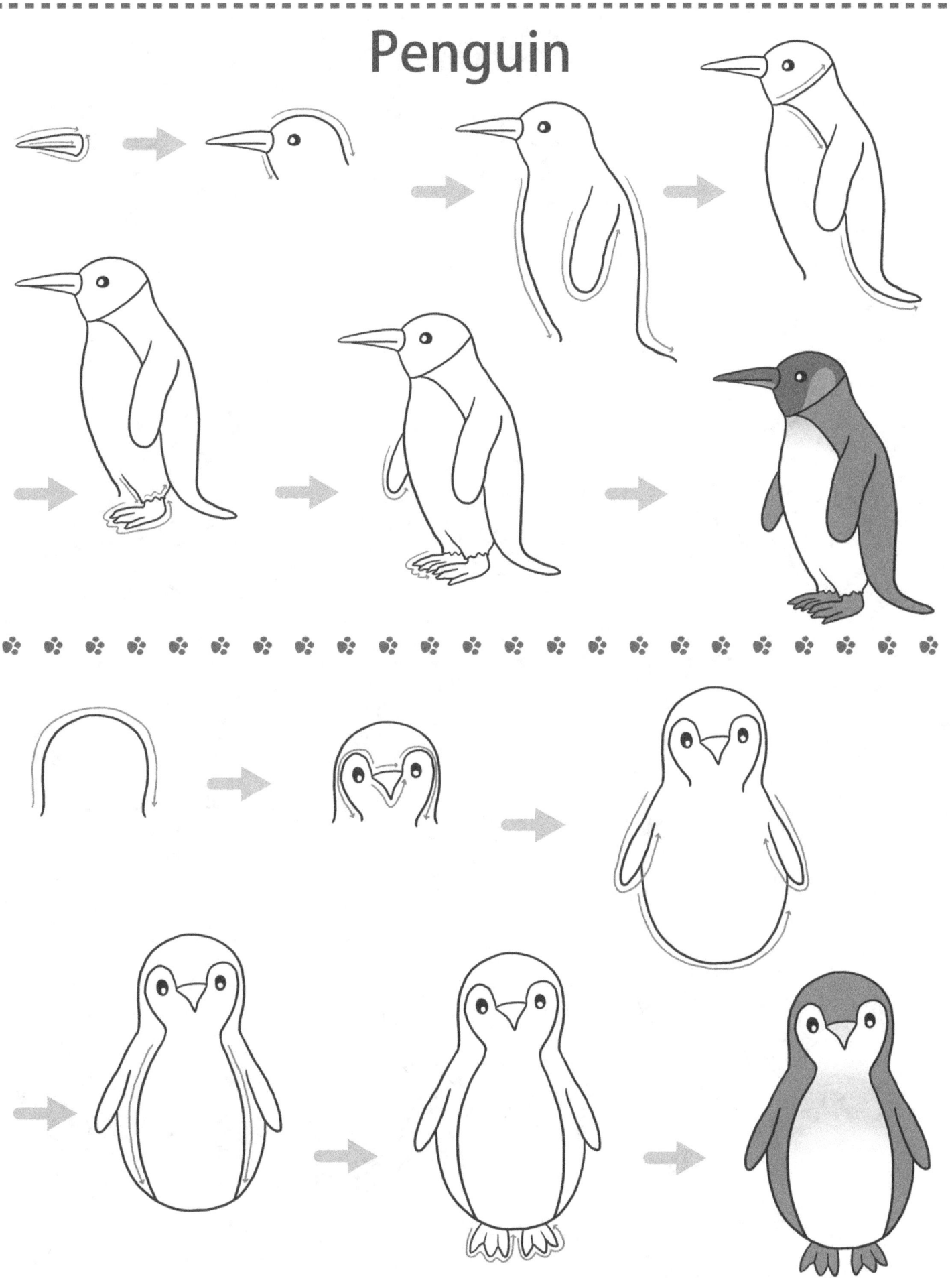

Pigeon

Parrot

Eagle

Vulture

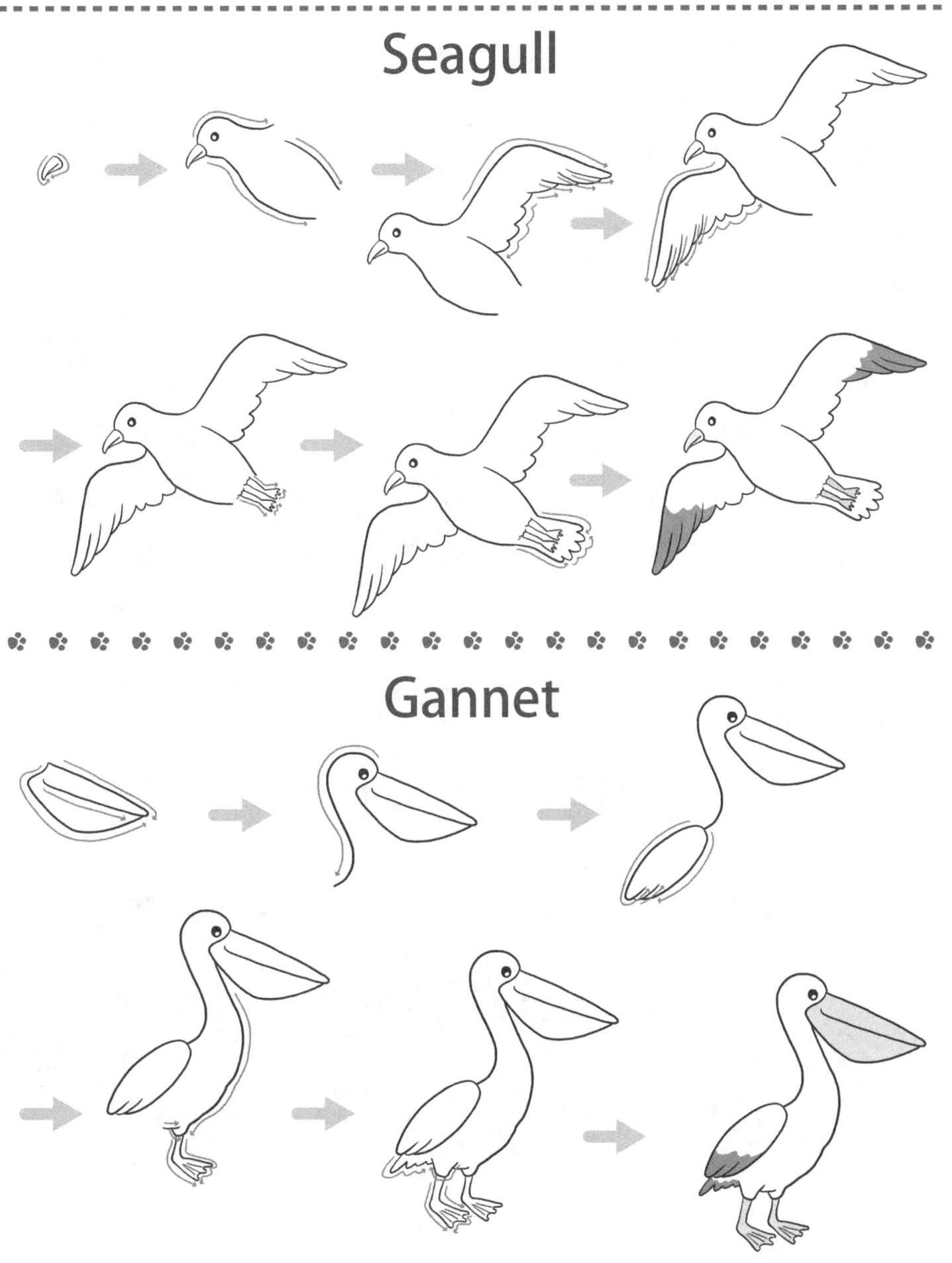

Ostrich

Peacock

Crocodile

Snake

Turtle

Lizard

Frog

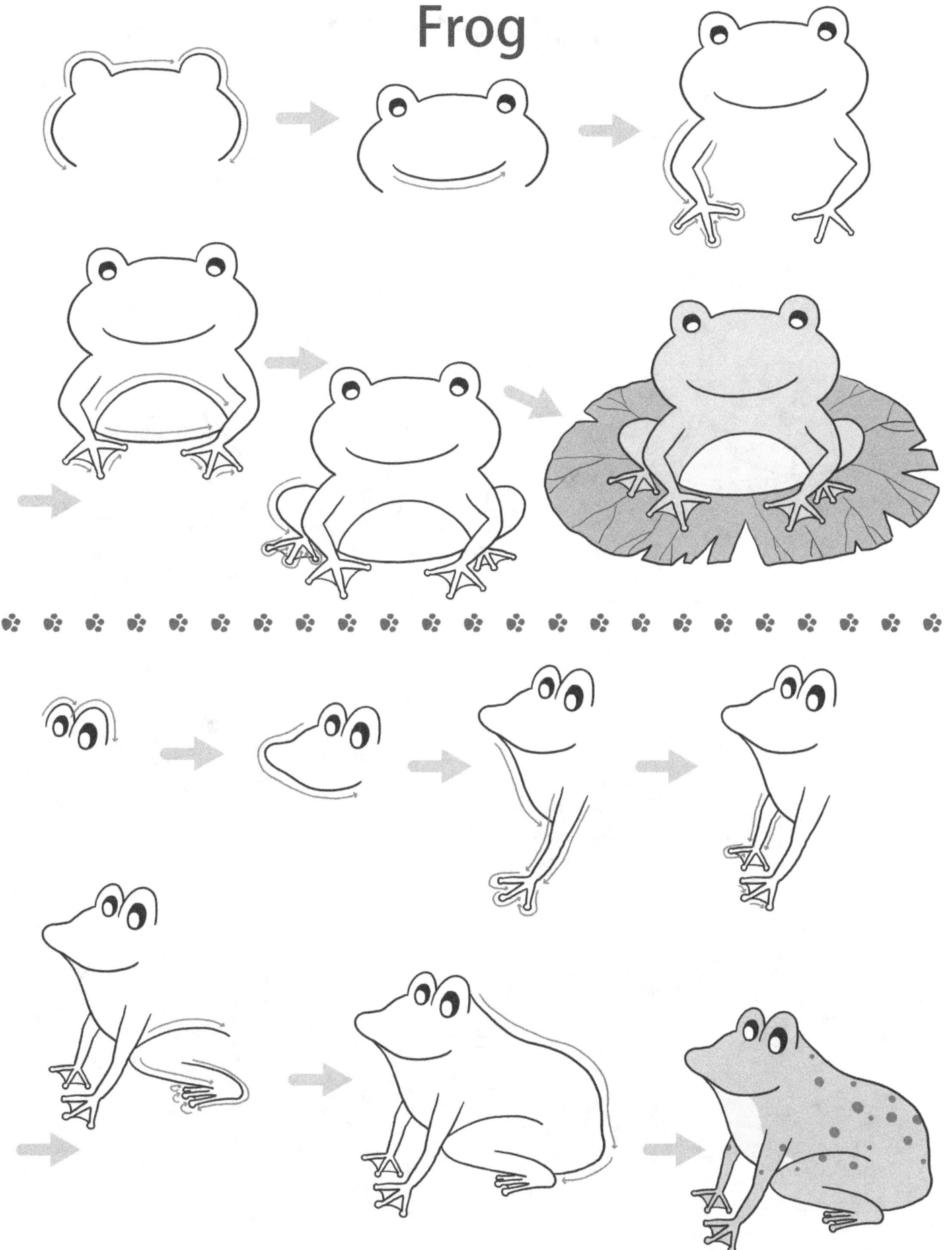

Goldfish

Fish

Pufferfish

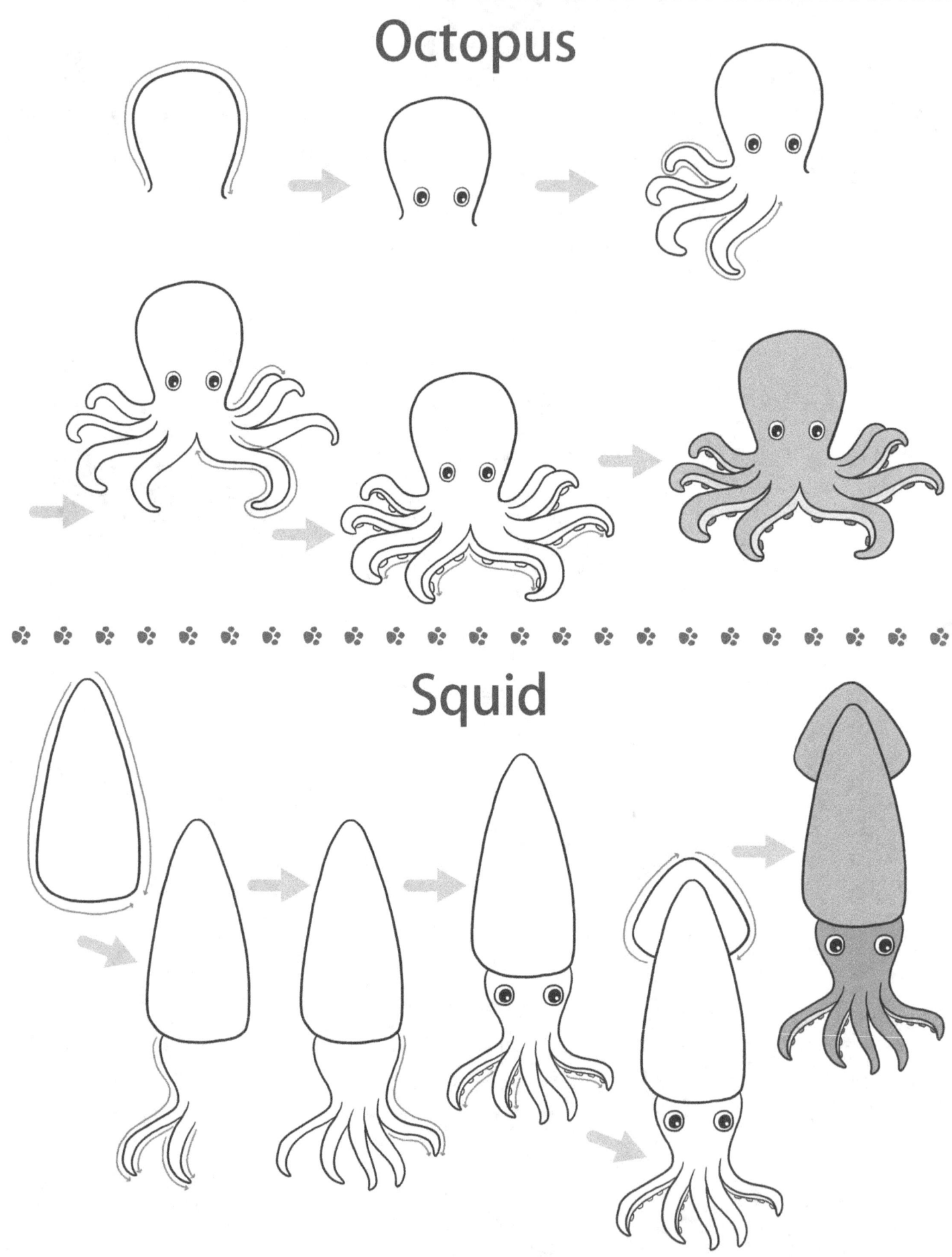

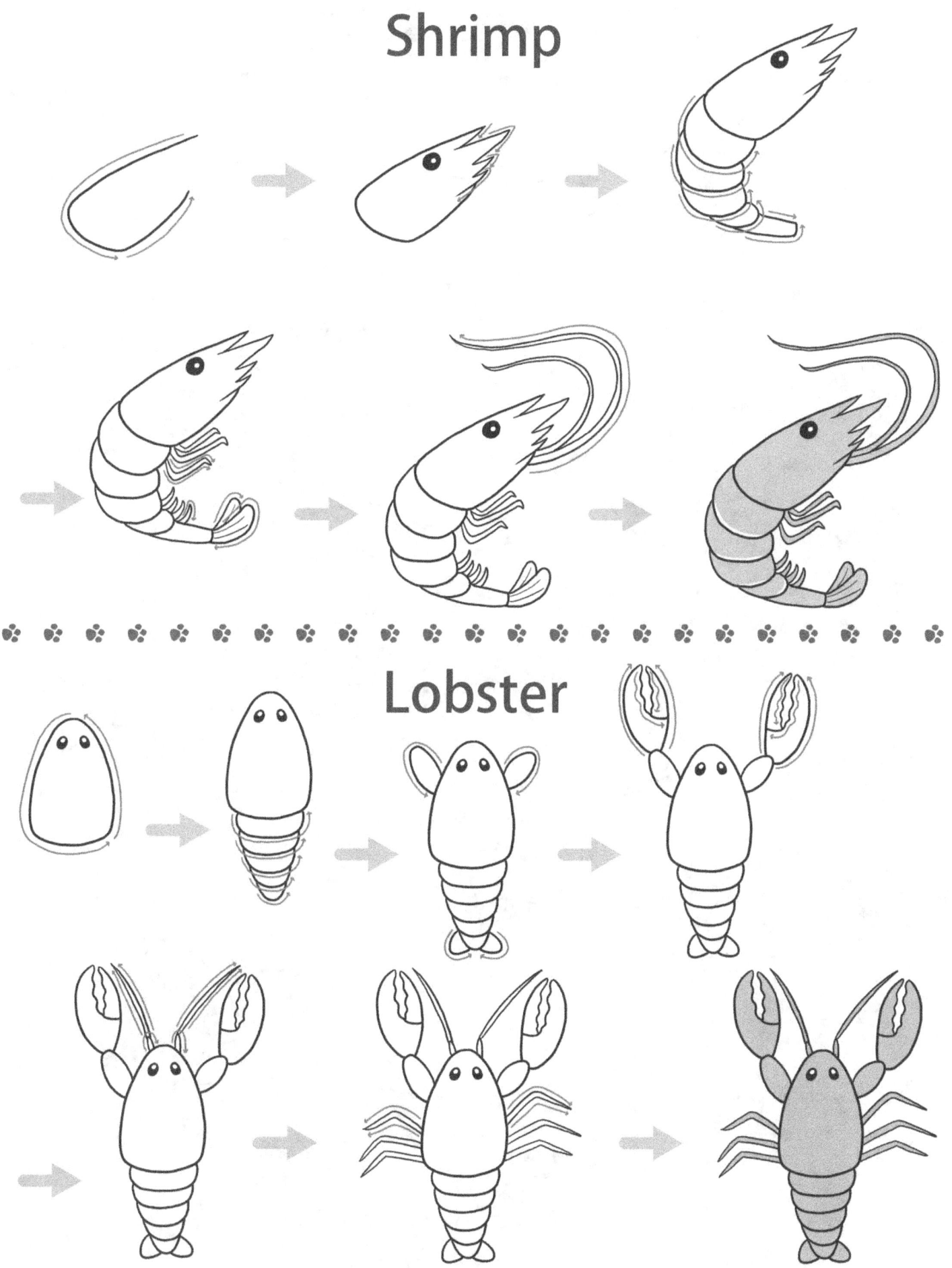

Seahorse

Jellyfish

Shellfish

Snail

Ladybug

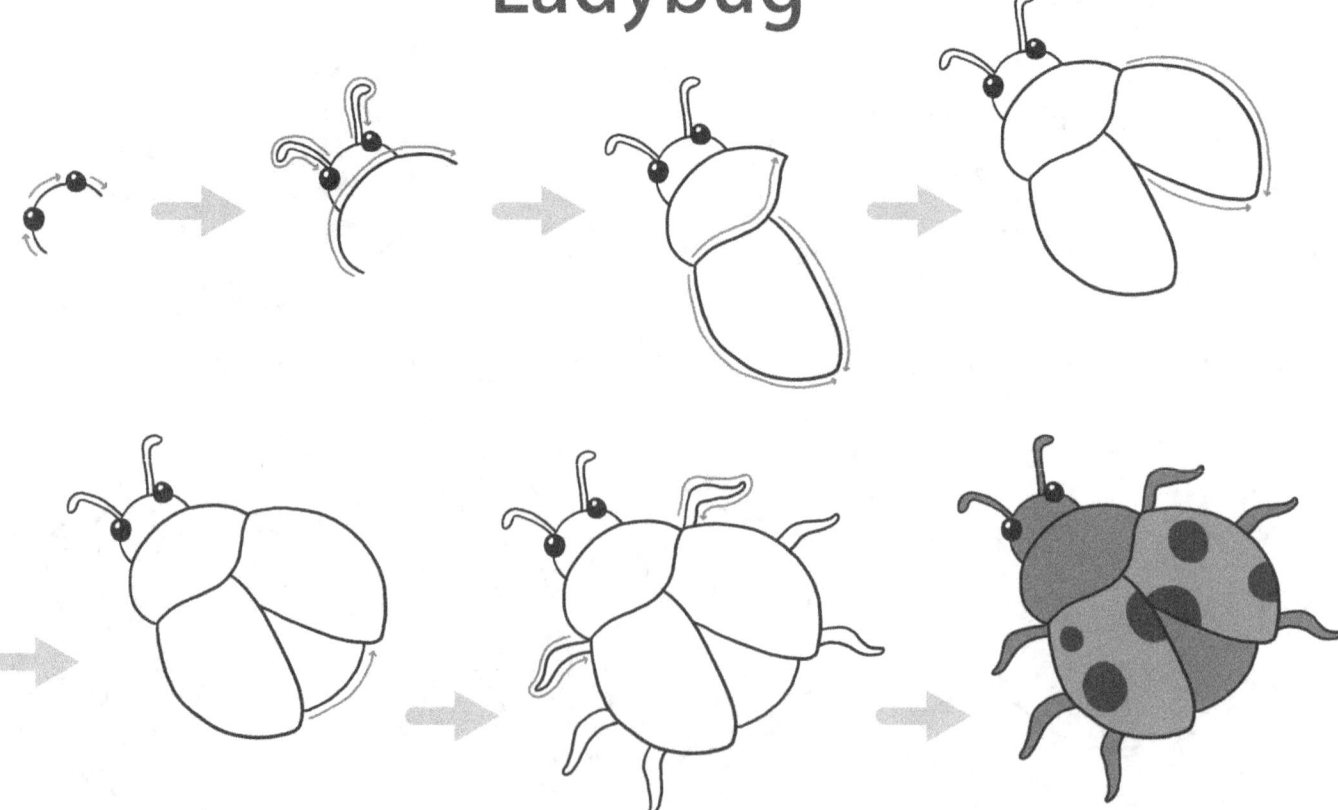

Butterfly

Bee

Dragonfly

www.ingramcontent.com/pod-product-compliance
Lightning Source LLC
Chambersburg PA
CBHW080909220526
45466CB00011BA/3523